Life As ...

Life As a Prospector in the California Gold Rush

Kate Shoup

Cavendish Square
New York

Published in 2017 by Cavendish Square Publishing, LLC
243 5th Avenue, Suite 136, New York, NY 10016

First Edition

Names: Shoup, Kate, 1972- author.
Title: Life as a prospector in the California Gold Rush / Kate Shoup.
Description: New York : Cavendish Square Publishing, [2017] | Series: Life as... | Includes index. | Description based on print version record and CIP data provided by publisher; resource not viewed.
Identifiers: LCCN 2015048467 (print) | LCCN 2015047445 (ebook) | ISBN 9781502617682 (ebook) | ISBN 9781502617903 (pbk.) | ISBN 9781502617804 (library bound) | ISBN 9781502617620 (6 pack)
Subjects: LCSH: California—Gold discoveries—Juvenile literature. | Gold miners—California—Juvenile literature. | Frontier and pioneer life—California—Juvenile literature. | California—History—1846-1850—Juvenile literature.
Classification: LCC F865 (print) | LCC F865 .S55155 2016 (ebook) | DDC 979.4/03--dc23
LC record available at http://lccn.loc.gov/2015048467

Editorial Director: David McNamara
Editor: Kristen Susienka
Copy Editor: Rebecca Rohan
Art Director: Jeffrey Talbot
Designer: Alan Sliwinski
Senior Production Manager: Jennifer Ryder-Talbot
Photo Research: J8 Media

The photographs in this book are used by permission and through the courtesy of: Everett Historical/Shutterstock.com, cover; American Photographer, (19th century)/Private Collection/Peter Newark American Pictures/Bridgeman Images, 4; File:Historic American Buildings Survey Sacramento Chamber of Commerce Original-1851(Drawing) Re-photo- April 1940 GENERAL VIEW - Sutter's Mill, American River (submerged), Coloma, HABSCAL,9-COLO.V,1-2.tif/Wikimedia Commons, 6; File:James Marshall2.jpg/Wikimedia Commons, 9; Library of Congress, 10; Library of Congress, 13; Library of Congress, 14; Bruce Dale/National Geographic/Getty Images, 16; Hulton Archive/Getty Images, 19; Apic/Hulton Archive/Getty Images, 20; Hulton Archive/Getty Images, 21; American Photographer, (19th century)/Private Collection/Peter Newark American Pictures/Bridgeman Images, 22; GraphicaArtis/Getty Images, 23; File:SanFranciscoharbor1851c sharp.jpg/Wikimedia Commons, 24; File: Seal of California, Department of Education, 1430 N Street, Sacramento, California.jpg/Wikimedia Commons, 26.

Printed in the United States of America

Contents

Introduction

In 1848, a worker named James Marshall found gold in northern California. It was at a place called Sutter's Mill.

After that, many Americans caught "gold fever" and raced to the area to find gold. In total, more than three hundred thousand people moved to California to dig for gold. This period of time was called the California gold rush. It lasted until 1855.

During the California gold rush, anyone could become rich! People who searched for gold were called **prospectors**. Some prospectors did find gold. Others were not so lucky. Many were left penniless. Some died.

The California gold rush was an exciting time.

A prospector pans for gold during the California gold rush.

James Marshall found gold here, at Sutter's Mill.

Chapter 1

The Gold Rush Begins

On February 2, 1848, the United States signed a **treaty** with Mexico that ended the Mexican-American War. It was called the Treaty of Guadalupe Hidalgo. It said that Mexico had to give the United States a lot of land. This included California.

In 1848, California was not as crowded as it is today. About 12,000 white and Mexican settlers and 150,000 Native Americans lived there.

When Mexico and America signed the treaty, there was something they didn't know. Nine days earlier, James Marshall had found gold in California. Marshall was building a **sawmill** called Sutter's Mill on the American River. On January 24, 1848, Marshall was

Manifest Destiny

Before 1848, America was smaller than it is today. Some people wanted America to spread west, all the way to the Pacific Ocean. The belief that this should happen was called **manifest destiny**. When Mexico gave its land to the United States, manifest destiny became real. The country stretched "from sea to shining sea."

working on the sawmill when he saw some glittering rocks on the ground on the side of the river. The rocks were gold!

Marshall told his boss, John Sutter, about the gold. At first, the two men tried to keep the gold a secret. But by May 1848, the secret was out. Soon, prospectors would arrive from all over the world. The California gold rush had begun.

James Marshall. Although he was the first to find gold in California, he died a poor man.

Wagons travel the California Trail, the route from the eastern United States to California.

Chapter 2

Prospectors Flock to California

At first, nobody outside of California knew about the gold. There was no telegraph line or railroad to link California with the rest of the country. News from California traveled by ship or by horseback.

In September 1848, people in the eastern United States started hearing stories about the gold. At first, nobody believed them. But then, in December 1848, US president James K. Polk said that the stories were true. After that, people left their jobs, packed up their belongings, and went to California to become prospectors. Most of these prospectors were men. Many left their families behind.

In 1849, eighty thousand prospectors arrived in California. Even more came after that. These men were called **forty-niners**. About half of the forty-niners traveled by sea. The other half traveled over land. They followed a route called the California Trail. Some people on the California Trail rode in covered wagons. Others rode mules or horses. Still others simply walked.

The trip by sea was long. It took more than six months. The trip by land was shorter. It took between three and four months. But it was more dangerous. Travelers had to cross mountains and deserts to get to California. Many died along the way.

The California Trail

The California Trail was 2,000 miles (3,218 kilometers) long. It began in Missouri, then crossed Nebraska, Wyoming, Idaho, Utah, and Nevada. Finally, it ended in Northern California.

Sam Brannan

Some people found gold by digging for it. Others "struck gold" in other ways. Sam Brannan was one of these people. Instead of digging for gold, Brannan opened a store near Sutter's Mill. There, he sold all the tools a prospector might need. Brannan became California's first millionaire.

The life of the prospector was hard, and the living conditions were primitive.

Chapter 3

The Life of a Prospector

The first prospectors arrived in Sutter's Mill in May 1848. Most came from San Francisco, about 140 miles (225 km) away. These first prospectors were lucky. They didn't have to dig for gold. They could just pick it up from the ground! Many of these early prospectors became very rich. Some earned thousands of dollars per day!

Before long, all the easy-to-find gold was gone. After that, prospectors started **panning** for gold in rivers and streams. This was harder than picking up gold from the ground. As more and more prospectors arrived, the gold in the rivers also became scarce. Soon, prospectors had to

At first, prospectors could simply pick up gold from the ground!

dig for gold. This was hard and tiring work. Worse, there was no guarantee of actually *finding* gold. Many prospectors quickly went broke.

Sometimes, prospectors teamed up to find gold. They formed large camps. These camps were lawless places. They had names like "Rough and Ready" and "Hangtown." After a long day at work, prospectors often relaxed in the camps. They sang and danced. They drank and played cards. Sometimes they fought.

There were no houses in these camps. Most prospectors lived in wagons, tents, or small wooden buildings called shanties. Some simply slept on the ground. This was not so bad in the summer. In the winter, things were worse. It was cold. Snow fell. Some prospectors froze to death.

The food was terrible. Fruit and vegetables were difficult to find. Food was also expensive. A single egg or slice of bread cost $1. That equals $27 today. Many prospectors could not afford this. They were forced to eat rotten bacon, old beef jerky, and beans. Because they did not have good food to eat, many prospectors became sick. Some died.

The work was difficult. The camps were harsh. The food was bad. But perhaps worse than any of

Daily Schedule of a Prospector

Before sunrise	Wake up and eat breakfast
Sunrise	Begin work
Noon	Eat lunch
Afternoon	Continue working
Sunset	Stop work and return to camp
Evening	Eat dinner and relax
9 p.m.	Go to bed

that was the loneliness that many prospectors felt. Most prospectors had left their families behind in search of their fortune. They wrote many letters home. In time, if they had enough money, some prospectors sent for their wives and children. However, most prospectors could not afford to do so.

Some prospectors teamed up and formed camps, like this one.

Prospectors used rockers to find gold in the gravel in riverbeds.

Chapter 4

A Prospector's Tools

Prospectors bought many supplies when they arrived in California. They needed some items just to survive, like a blanket, a tent, and food. If they had a little extra money, prospectors might also buy a lamp, a kettle for making tea, and a baking pan.

To find gold, each prospector needed a shovel and a pick. They might also buy a hatchet, a gardening hoe, and a pail. Perhaps most importantly, they needed a wide, shallow pan. Prospectors used these pans

Prospectors with their mining equipment.

Prospectors use a long tom.

to scoop up gravel along a river or stream. Then they shook the pan in the water. Any gold in the gravel would settle to the bottom of the pan.

Prospectors invented a tool called a **rocker**. This was a wooden device that looked like a cradle, with lots of small holes in the bottom. With a rocker, three prospectors could work together to process more gravel. One prospector used a shovel to dig up gravel and put it in the rocker. Another prospector carried buckets of water from a nearby river or stream to the rocker. A third prospector poured the water into the rocker and rocked it back and forth to separate the gold from the gravel. After rockers, someone invented long toms. These were similar to rockers, but larger. They could process even more gravel.

Working the Rocker

One prospector recalled carrying three hundred buckets of dirt to a rocker in one day. This yielded $75 in gold—more than $2,000 today. The sum was split evenly among the three men working the rocker. "Not bad," the prospector said, "but not as good as the work should have produced."

What did prospectors do with the gold they found? At first, they used it like money to pay for things. Soon, local businessmen built banks. There, prospectors could exchange gold for paper money. Some gold was sent back east. Usually, gold was transported by **stagecoach**. Not surprisingly, stagecoaches were frequent targets for bandits along the route.

Prospectors sent gold back east on stagecoaches.

San Francisco around 1850.

Chapter 5

The Impact of the Gold Rush

The California gold rush lasted until 1855. That's when the gold ran out. However, even though the gold was gone, California remained an important part of the United States.

The California gold rush forever changed the lives of all the prospectors who searched for gold. Some prospectors were successful and became very rich. Others never found anything. After 1855, many prospectors stayed in California and became farmers. Because so many prospectors moved to California, Congress made it a state in 1850. Today, more people live in California than in any other state.

The state seal of California shows a prospector in the background.

The gold rush did not only change the lives of prospectors. It also affected many Native American people living in the West. Before 1848, there were far more Native Americans than settlers. Soon, many settlers moved onto Native American land. Many Native Americans died during the gold rush era. Some died from diseases the settlers brought. Others were killed by settlers, who were afraid of Native Americans. After the gold rush, there were more settlers than Native Americans living in California.

The gold rush still is very important to California. A prospector is shown on the state seal. The state's nickname is "The Golden State." State highway signs are shaped like a prospector's shovel. Many museums have exhibits about the gold rush. The exhibits tell people's stories, show prospectors' tools, and display photographs of what it was like to live during this time. The gold rush will always be remembered in the history of California and the United States.

Glossary

forty-niners People who moved to California in 1849 in search of gold.

manifest destiny A belief that it is America's duty to expand its territory and spread its way of life.

panning A mining technique in which a wide, shallow pan is used to scoop up gravel alongside (or under) a river or stream and then shaken in the water to sift out the gold.

prospector who searches for minerals such as gold. Also called a miner.

rocker A simple wooden device used to process gravel and find gold.

sawmill A machine that cuts logs into lumber.

stagecoach A carriage pulled by horses to transport passengers and goods.

treaty An agreement between two or more countries.

Find Out More

Books

Holub, Joan. *What Was the Gold Rush?* New York: Grosset & Dunlap, 2013.

Raum, Elizabeth. *The California Gold Rush: An Interactive History Adventure*. Mankato, MN: Capstone Press, 2007.

Schanzer, Rosalyn. *Gold Fever: Tales from the California Gold Rush*. Washington, DC: National Geographic Children's Books, 2006.

Website

The Gold Rush by PBS

www.pbs.org/wgbh/amex/goldrush/index.html

Video

The Gold Rush of 1849

www.history.com/topics/gold-rush-of-1849

Index

Page numbers in **boldface** are illustrations. Entries in **boldface** are glossary terms.

About the Author

Kate Shoup has written more than thirty books and has edited hundreds more. When not working, Kate loves to ski, read, ride her motorcycle, and watch IndyCar racing. She lives in Indianapolis with her husband, her daughter, and their dog.